EXPLORING SCIENCE

THE GREENHOUSE EFFECT

WARMING THE PLANET

BY DARLENE R. STILLE

Content Adviser: Robert Davis, Ph.D., Associate Professor of
Environmental Sciences, University of Virginia

Science Adviser: Terrence E. Young Jr., M.Ed., M.L.S.,
Jefferson Parish (Louisiana) Public School System

Reading Adviser: Rosemary G. Palmer, Ph.D., Department of Literacy,
College of Education, Boise State University

 COMPASS POINT BOOKS · MINNEAPOLIS, MINNESOTA

Compass Point Books • 3109 West 50th Street, #115 • Minneapolis, MN 55410

Visit Compass Point Books on the Internet at *www.compasspointbooks.com*
or e-mail your request to *custserv@compasspointbooks.com*

Photographs ©: Jaime Martens, cover; Digital Stock, 4; Mohsin Raza/Reuters/Corbis, 5; Shutter-stock/Robert Mizerek, 7; James Leynes/Corbis, 8; Shutterstock/Vladimir Pomortzeff, 9; Shutter-stock/Dennis Sabo, 10; Digital Vision, 11; Shutterstock/Michael Schofield, 13; Shutterstock/Clara Natoli, 15; Shutterstock/Dmitry Pichugin, 16; Shutterstock/Jim Parkin, 17; Pakistan Tourism Office/Handout/Reuters/Corbis, 18; Shutterstock/Wojciech, 22–23; Ardea/Edizioni White Star, 24; Bostjan Fele/Reuters/Corbis, 25; Ashley Cooper/Corbis, 29; Shutterstock/Darren Hedges, 30; The Granger Collection, New York, 31; Yogi Inc./Corbis, 32; David Muench/Corbis, 33; ENEA/Handout/Reuters/Corbis, 34; PhotoDisc, 35; Galen Rowell/Corbis, 36; Shutterstock/Silense, 37, 40, 44; Bo Zaunders/Corbis, 42; Shutterstock/Brian Stewart-Coxon, 43; Shut-terstock/Pieter Janssen, 46.

Editor: Anthony Wacholtz
Designer/Page Production: The Design Lab
Photo Researcher: Lori Bye
Cartographer: XNR Productions, Inc.
Illustrators: Eric Hoffmann and Farhana Hossain

Art Director: Jaime Martens
Creative Director: Keith Griffin
Editorial Director: Carol Jones
Managing Editor: Catherine Neitge

Library of Congress Cataloging-in-Publication Data
Stille, Darlene R.
    The greenhouse effect : warming the planet / by Darlene R. Stille.
        p. cm. — (Exploring science)
    Includes index.
    ISBN-13: 978-0-7565-1956-8 (hardcover)
    ISBN-10: 0-7565-1956-X (hardcover)
    1. Greenhouse effect, Atmospheric. 2. Global warming. 3. Climatology. I. Title.
    II. Series.
    QC912.3.S75 2006
    363.738'74—dc22   2006006763

About the Author

Darlene R. Stille is a science writer and author of more than 80 books for young people. She grew up in Chicago and attended the University of Illinois, where she discovered her love of writing. She has received numerous awards for her work. She lives and writes in Michigan.

TABLE OF CONTENTS

Is Earth Growing Warmer?

THE HEAT AND HUMIDITY in Chicago were stifling during the summer of 1995. A terrible heat wave began on July 13, when the temperature soared to 106 degrees Fahrenheit (41 degrees Celsius). For the next week, temperatures hovered between the high 90s and low 100s. The high humidity made the situation even worse.

The city of Chicago was overwhelmed by a heat wave in the summer of 1995.

The heat index, a measurement that combines temperature and humidity, showed that the air on a person's skin actually felt like 120 F (49 C).

The Chicago heat wave did more than just make people feel uncomfortable—it was a killer. By some estimates, more than 700 people died from heat-related conditions, especially elderly or sick people who were confined to homes without air conditioning. An even worse death toll occurred in Europe in August 2003. A record-breaking heat wave was blamed for approximately 35,000 deaths.

People in Lahore, Pakistan, took refuge in a canal in May 2005 when temperatures reached 111 F (44 C).

Although there have always been summer heat waves, periods of extremely hot weather have become more frequent. Many scientists believe that the increase in summer heat waves could be a result of Earth growing warmer. The 10 warmest years of the 20th century were between 1985 and 2000, with 1998 being the warmest on record.

GETTING HOTTER

There have always been changes in the temperature of the atmosphere. These changes have happened naturally over millions of years. Places on Earth have gone from having a mild, wet climate to having the cold, snowy climate of an ice age. As the temperature decreased, forests and meadows were buried under huge rivers of ice called glaciers. When the temperature increased, glaciers retreated and forests and meadows returned. Ancient climate changes were due to a number of complex natural causes. Scientists have evidence, however, that the present warming trend is greater than any that could result from natural causes alone.

WHAT'S HEATING THE PLANET?

A buildup of certain gases is causing Earth to grow warmer, according to many scientists who study climate. These gases, called greenhouse gases, trap infrared radiation from Earth,

which originally came from the sun. Greenhouse gases include methane, water vapor, and carbon dioxide.

Earth needs a certain amount of greenhouse gases to stay warm enough to support life. However, carbon dioxide and other gases produced by factories, electric power plants,

Lush forests were in abundance during interglacial periods, the time between ice ages.

and automobile exhausts are adding greatly to the amount of greenhouse gases in the atmosphere.

A rise in the amount of greenhouse gases in the atmosphere since the late 1800s corresponds to an increase in global temperature. Some scientists are concerned that if greenhouse gases continue to be added to the atmosphere by human activities, the global warming could cause serious problems. Some scientists believe that changes in precipitation patterns may cause some regions to become deserts, while other areas could

The rise in the number of automobiles in the world has produced more greenhouse gases in the atmosphere.

vanish under rising seas or be washed away by floodwaters.

There are many uncertainties, however, about what is going on with the climate. Scientists cannot predict what will happen to a particular region if people continue to send huge quantities of pollutants into the air. Scientists and governments worldwide are calling for more studies to determine the effects of excess greenhouse gases in the atmosphere and what people can do to prevent serious consequences.

Some scientists believe that more deserts could develop from lack of rainfall.

CHAPTER TWO

⊕ A Perfect Planet

LEAVING A FIERY trail behind it, a rocket blasts off from its launching pad. The rocket is carrying a space probe to a distant planet. The probe flies around the planet, taking pictures of its surface and measuring the gases in its atmosphere. A robot lander detaches from the probe and parachutes down to the planet's surface. Instruments aboard the lander analyze soil and air samples, looking for signs of life. The lander radios its findings back to Earth.

Since the Space Age began in 1957, spacecraft have visited our moon and many of the planets in our solar system. Spacecraft have landed on the moon, Mars, and Venus. Voyager space probes and other craft have flown around Mercury, Saturn, Jupiter, and many of their moons. The Voyager probes have even flown by the distant planets of Neptune and Uranus. The powerful Hubble Space Telescope has snapped pictures of Pluto, the most distant known planet from the sun.

TOO HOT, TOO COLD, JUST RIGHT

Astronomers studied the pictures and analyzed the measurements for signs of

Rockets and space probes have explored our solar system and collected data, allowing us to compare Earth to other planets.

life. From the collected data, they were able to determine that the surface temperature of Mercury can rise to a sizzling 800 F (430 C) during the day but drop to minus 280 F (minus 170 C) at night. The temperature of Mars ranges from minus 60 to minus 230 F (minus 20 to minus 140 C). The outer planets—Jupiter, Saturn, Uranus, and Neptune—are made up entirely of atmosphere and have no solid, rocky surfaces. They are so far from the sun that their temperatures are hundreds of degrees below zero. Little is known about distant Pluto other than it is a ball of ice. The data, however, did not provide any evidence of life on any moon or planet other than Earth.

Conditions on Earth today make it the perfect planet to support life in our solar system. The atmosphere contains just the right balance of gases to support life. It is made up mainly of nitrogen (78 percent) and oxygen (21 percent). Other gases, such as argon, carbon dioxide, methane, and water vapor, make up the other 1 percent.

The Hubble Space Telescope orbits Earth, taking photographs from space.

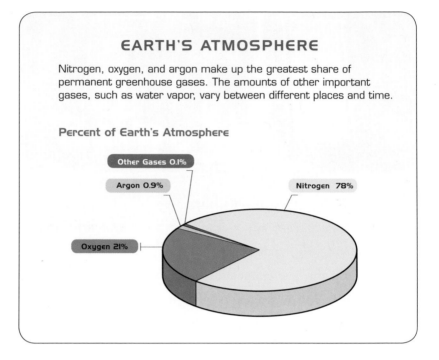

EARTH'S ATMOSPHERE

Nitrogen, oxygen, and argon make up the greatest share of permanent greenhouse gases. The amounts of other important gases, such as water vapor, vary between different places and time.

Percent of Earth's Atmosphere

- Other Gases 0.1%
- Argon 0.9%
- Nitrogen 78%
- Oxygen 21%

Scientists divide Earth's atmosphere into several layers, which extend far above Earth's surface until they trail off into space. The lowest and densest layer is the troposphere, which goes up about 5 to 9 miles (8 to 14.5 kilometers) from Earth's surface. Beyond that is the stratosphere, which reaches about 31 miles (50 km) above Earth's surface. Beyond the stratosphere are layers called the mesosphere and the thermosphere. Earth's atmosphere controls the climate for the entire planet. Other planets do not have such an ideal atmosphere. As a result, they are either too hot or too cold to support life.

How Earth's Atmosphere Formed

Scientists believe that Earth formed about 4.5 billion years ago from a cloud of dust and gas around the sun. At first, Earth was a waterless ball of rock surrounded by an atmosphere made up of hydrogen, helium, methane, and ammonia gases. Some scientists believe that Earth's early atmosphere also contained a large amount of carbon dioxide but no oxygen. How did the atmosphere change?

There is a theory that the early Earth was very hot inside. The heat came from radioactive decay of certain elements and from the force of gravity pulling metals toward the center of the planet. The heat melted rocks and created many volcanoes. The lava, or melted rock, shooting out of volcanoes gave off gases, including oxygen, which became part of the early atmosphere.

Over millions of years, Earth's atmosphere evolved until it contained a mixture of gases. Only 0.1 percent of the atmosphere is made up of carbon dioxide and other greenhouse gases. This small amount of greenhouse gases is enough to make Earth's temperature just right to sustain life.

Steam billows from lava that has erupted from a volcano and poured into the ocean.

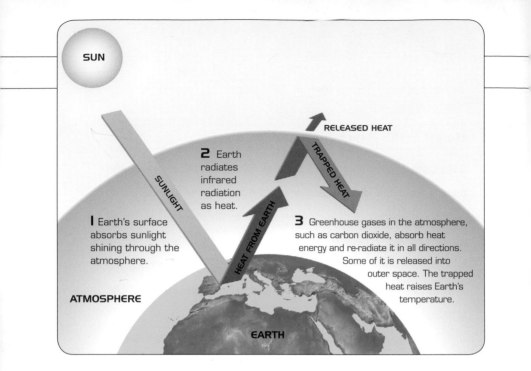

SUN

2 Earth radiates infrared radiation as heat.

RELEASED HEAT

TRAPPED HEAT

SUNLIGHT

HEAT FROM EARTH

1 Earth's surface absorbs sunlight shining through the atmosphere.

3 Greenhouse gases in the atmosphere, such as carbon dioxide, absorb heat energy and re-radiate it in all directions. Some of it is released into outer space. The trapped heat raises Earth's temperature.

ATMOSPHERE

EARTH

EARTH'S NATURAL GREENHOUSE EFFECT

Greenhouse gases play a critical role in regulating a planet's "thermostat" through what scientists call the greenhouse effect. The greenhouse effect got its name because scientists compared the warming of Earth's atmosphere to the way a greenhouse warms the plants inside it. Although the name remains, scientists have decided the comparison is not quite accurate.

Earth's natural greenhouse effect is a complex system. Only about 50 percent of the sun's energy that reaches Earth penetrates down to the surface. The atmosphere reflects about 30 percent of the incoming solar rays and absorbs another 20 percent. Earth's surface absorbs some of the incoming rays and radiates back heat, or infrared rays. Gas molecules and particles in the clouds and atmosphere absorb some of the radiated heat from Earth's surface. The warmed molecules and particles then radiate heat in all directions. Some of it goes into space, and some of it goes back to the ground.

This heat energy bouncing back and forth keeps most places on Earth at a temperature where life can survive. There are extreme temperatures at some places on Earth. The highest temperature ever recorded, 136 F (58 C), was in a Middle Eastern desert, and the record low, minus 128.6 F (minus 89.6 C), was in Antarctica. Earth's average surface temperature is 59 F (15 C), but without the natural greenhouse effect, it would only be 0 F (minus 18 C).

The highest temperature on Earth was recorded in a desert in the Middle East.

What's the Difference Between Weather and Climate?

WE TUNE IN to the radio or television to hear the weather forecast. Will tomorrow be a rainy or sunny day? Does the long-range weather forecast call for a colder-than-usual winter or a hotter-than-usual summer? Weather comes from the atmosphere, mainly the lower part called the troposphere. Weather is a combination of the conditions in the atmosphere at a particular place and time.

Just as a thunderstorm can develop quickly, the weather can change within a matter of minutes.

Climate is the weather at a particular place over long periods of time. Climatologists say that deserts, such as those in the Southwestern United States, have an arid, or dry, climate. In an arid climate, there is very little water vapor in the air and very little rainfall. Southern Florida and the islands in the Caribbean Sea have a tropical climate, which is warm and humid all year long. Climatologists call the climate in the central and Midwestern United States a temperate climate. There are four seasons in a temperate climate area, with warm summers and cold winters.

WHY DO DIFFERENT PLACES HAVE DIFFERENT CLIMATES?

There are several reasons why different places on Earth have different climates. One reason is that the

The arid climate of a desert allows cacti to flourish year round.

sun's rays do not strike all places on Earth equally. Most rays strike areas near the equator, an imaginary line around the middle of the planet. The fewest rays strike areas near the cold North and South poles.

Why are mountains often capped with snow? Climate varies with altitude, or how high a place is above sea level. The higher the altitude, the cooler the climate. Because high mountains have a cool climate, snow remains on the mountaintops for most or all of the year. Mountains can also affect

K-2, the second highest mountain in the world, is part of the Himalayan range.

rainfall. Winds, which blow from the west in the Northern Hemisphere, carry water vapor that rose from the Pacific Ocean. The winds blow up the mountain, cooling the water vapor and forming clouds. Rain or snow falls on the western slope of the mountain. Winds blowing down the eastern side of the mountain become warmer the farther down they go. The water vapor and clouds disappear, and there is less rain or snow.

A location's distance from an ocean or large lake can also affect the climate. Areas near bodies of water have more heat-trapping water vapor than areas that are far inland. Wind patterns also affect climate by distributing heat and precipitation in certain areas.

HOW CLIMATE CAN CHANGE

The climates of various regions on Earth have changed many times. Several things can cause climate change, including drifting continents, changes in Earth's orbit, energy output of the sun, and volcanic eruptions.

Fossils of ancient organisms hold clues to past climate change. For example, scientists have found fossils of tropical plants near the North Pole, indicating that this cold region was once very warm. Such radical climate change was caused by continental drift. Earth's crust is made up of 14 gigantic plates

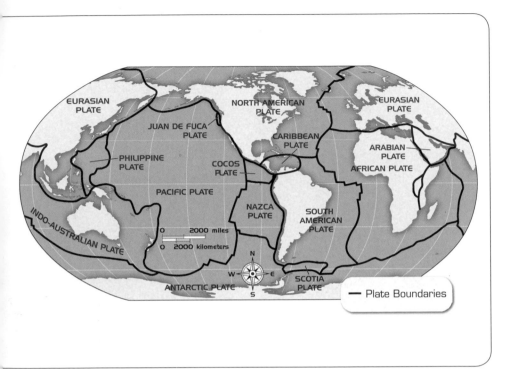

of rock. These rigid tectonic plates move around on flowing hot rock below. Geologists believe that all the continents were once part of a huge landmass they call Pangaea. As the plates moved, they carried the continents with them. What is now the Arctic was once close to the equator, and tropical plants grew there. Climate change caused by continental drift took millions of years.

Another reason for past changes in Earth's climate is Earth's orbit. Changes in Earth's orbit around the sun can

Earth's crust is divided into 14 major tectonic plates.

make the global climate grow colder or warmer over periods lasting between 23,000 and 100,000 years. Scientists believe that Earth's distance from the sun and the way in which the planet tilts as it travels around the sun brought on several ice ages. Huge sheets of ice called glaciers crept over large parts of the planet during these periods. The first ice age may have occurred more than 2 billion years ago. The latest ice age ended about 11,500 years ago. Scientists believe that an ice

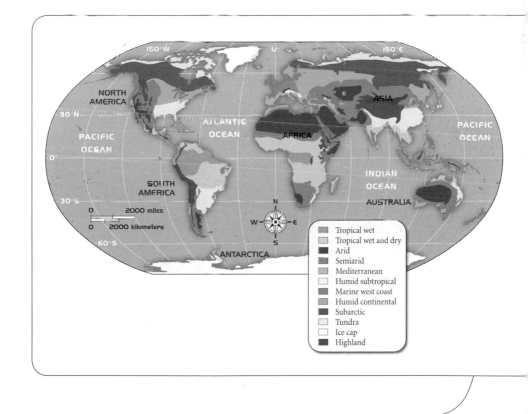

A region's climate depends on its location on Earth.

How Climate Is Created

The global climate of a planet depends on how far it is from the sun, what kinds of gases make up its atmosphere, and what its mass is. A planet's mass determines how well its force of gravity can hold gases in place around the planet.

Mercury, the closest planet to the sun, has almost no atmosphere to help control its temperatures. Pluto, the farthest planet from the sun, receives the least solar energy and is freezing cold.

Mars has an atmosphere made up largely of carbon dioxide, a greenhouse gas that traps heat. However, the atmosphere of Mars is thin because the planet does not have enough mass to hold an atmosphere in place through

the force of gravity. Venus has about the same amount of mass as Earth, but the atmosphere is 95 percent carbon dioxide, which traps so much heat that the planet's temperature averages 860 F (460 C).

In addition to how much solar heat and light energy reaches it, a planet's climate also depends on how much of the sunlight is reflected back into space. For example, white cloud tops and large areas of snow and ice are good reflectors of heat and can keep a planet cooler.

The tops of clouds keep Earth cooler by reflecting heat from the sun.

age lasts about 100,000 years. The time between ice ages is called an interglacial period. These periods last from 10,000 to 20,000 years.

Other periods of climate change have been much shorter. From 1645 to 1715, during a period called the Little Ice Age, Europe was much colder than it is today. Scientists suspect that sunspots—cooler, darker areas on the sun—could have been responsible. Scientists are trying to determine if there is a connection between sunspot activity and Earth's climate and weather.

Woolly mammoths are some of the only animals that could survive during an ice age.

Volcanic eruptions have caused Earth's temperature to cool as well. Huge volcanic eruptions have given off enough dust and ash to block the sun's rays, causing global cooling for a few years. Changes in patterns of cold and warm water circulating in the ocean can also cause short-term climate change in certain places.

Additionally, the amount of carbon dioxide in the atmosphere can bring on climate change. There is a clear link between the amount of carbon dioxide in the atmosphere and global temperatures. Climate scientists have found that over the past 400,000 years, when carbon dioxide rose, temperatures also rose.

Mount Bromo, a volcano in Indonesia, billowed smoke, ash, and rocks the size of footballs.

Earth: The Great Recycler

Earth constantly recycles matter and energy. Some of these great worldwide cycles control weather and climate.

The water cycle is one of the most important cycles in weather and climate. Most of the water on Earth is in the ocean. Heat from the sun evaporates ocean water, which rises into the air as water vapor. The wind carries the water vapor over land, where it forms clouds and falls as precipitation. From the land, water drains into lakes and rivers, which flow back to the ocean. A single drop of water can go through the cycle over and over again. Because of this cycle, the amount of water on Earth always stays the same.

The carbon cycle is another important cycle. Algae and green plants are a vital part of the cycle. They take carbon dioxide from the air when they make food through the process of photosynthesis. As a waste product, they give off oxygen, which animals must breathe in order to stay alive. Animals give off carbon dioxide as a waste product. Plants and animals also release carbon dioxide when they die and decay.

Some carbon dioxide is "stored" in the fossil remains of plants and animals that died millions of years ago. Fossil fuels—such as coal, oil, and natural gas—were created from carbon deposits of prehistoric organisms, mainly plants. The stored carbon from these ancient organisms is released into

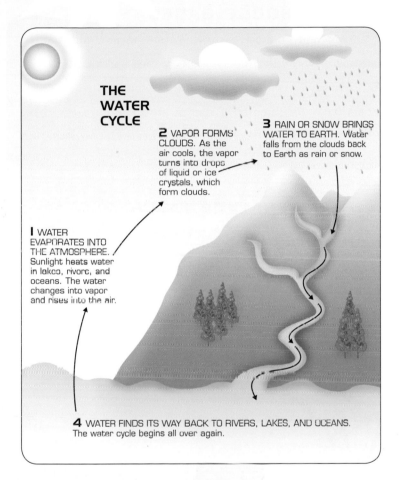

THE
WATER
CYCLE

2 VAPOR FORMS CLOUDS. As the air cools, the vapor turns into drops of liquid or ice crystals, which form clouds.

3 RAIN OR SNOW BRINGS WATER TO EARTH. Water falls from the clouds back to Earth as rain or snow.

1 WATER EVAPORATES INTO THE ATMOSPHERE. Sunlight heats water in lakes, rivers, and oceans. The water changes into vapor and rises into the air.

4 WATER FINDS ITS WAY BACK TO RIVERS, LAKES, AND OCEANS. The water cycle begins all over again.

the atmosphere when fossil fuels are burned. It is the release of this stored carbon dioxide from burning fossil fuels that scientists believe may be increasing the greenhouse effect and causing Earth's climate to grow warmer.

CHAPTER FOUR

The Runaway Greenhouse Effect

WHILE GREENHOUSE GASES are essential for life on Earth, too much greenhouse gas in the atmosphere could trap too much heat. Scientists call the excess of greenhouse gases in the atmosphere the "runaway" greenhouse effect.

Scientists have documented a rise in global temperature over the past 100 years. According to the Intergovernmental Panel on

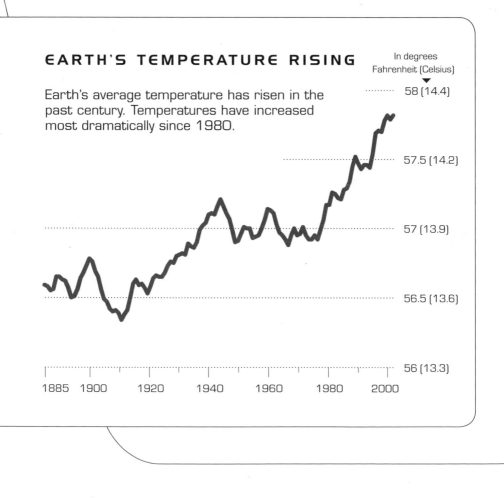

EARTH'S TEMPERATURE RISING

In degrees Fahrenheit (Celsius)

Earth's average temperature has risen in the past century. Temperatures have increased most dramatically since 1980.

58 (14.4)

57.5 (14.2)

57 (13.9)

56.5 (13.6)

56 (13.3)

1885   1900   1920   1940   1960   1980   2000

DID YOU KNOW?

The IPCC is a group formed in 1988 by the United Nations. The world's leading scientists attend meetings of this organization to discuss and evaluate all the evidence about increasing greenhouse gases and the possibility of global climate change.

Climate Change (IPCC), the average global temperature has risen about one degree since the mid-1800s. The greatest temperature increase occurred during the 1980s and 1990s. During this time, carbon dioxide in the atmosphere increased greatly.

THE RISE IN CO2

Many scientists believe that the carbon dioxide (CO_2) increase began with the Industrial Revolution in the middle 1700s and early 1800s. The Industrial Revolution was brought about by the invention of power-driven machines and a system of making goods in factories.

A chemical plant vents various gases into the atmosphere.

In 1769, a Scottish engineer named James Watt perfected the steam engine to make it drive machinery in factories. Steam engines required fuel to heat water for making steam that moved pistons and turned wheels to operate the machinery. At first, steam engines burned wood. Inventors and engineers learned, however, that coal burned more efficiently. During the 1800s, coal-fired steam engines were built to manufacture a wide range of goods. Steam engines were also used to power locomotives and steamships for hauling goods to places far away.

Smokestacks from factories, trains, and ships sent tons of pollution from the burning coal into the atmosphere. Among the pollutants were excessive amounts of CO_2 and other greenhouse gases.

By the late 1800s, the invention of other devices called for the burning of even more fossil fuels. American inventor Thomas A. Edison invented many electrical devices, including the incandescent lightbulb. In the 1880s, he began to build electric-generating power plants, which also burned coal.

James Watt's steam engine led to other inventions, such as the coal-powered steam locomotive.

Then a boiler that burned another fossil fuel, oil, came into use to power ships during World War I. The internal combustion engine, which burns gasoline, launched the Age of the Automobile.

Electricity, the automobile, and all kinds of manufactured goods greatly changed the lifestyle of people. Instead of traveling by horse and wagon, people could just hop into their cars. Instead of weaving cloth by firelight, a family could go to the store and buy coats and sweaters.

These goods also improved the health and increased the life span of people in countries that had advanced technologies. However, all of the devices that made life easier required power and the burning of a growing amount of gasoline, fuel oil, coal, and other fossil fuels. The burning of fossil fuels sent millions of tons of greenhouse gases into the atmosphere.

DID YOU KNOW?

The first big industry that came about because of the Industrial Revolution was the textile industry. Before factories, most families made whatever cloth they needed on looms in their homes.

Thomas A. Edison (1847–1931) built coal-burning power plants to create electricity.

CHAPTER FIVE

Studying the Greenhouse Effect

IN ORDER TO STUDY the greenhouse effect, scientists had to find ways of taking samples of Earth's atmosphere. They also had to find ways of learning what Earth's climate was like hundreds of thousands of years ago. They use these measurements and techniques to predict what might happen to the climate in the future.

MEASURING THE ATMOSPHERE

Meteorologists use weather balloons to study Earth's climate. Weather balloons carry instrument packages high up in the atmosphere to take various measurements, such as temperature. Orbiting weather satellites monitor temperature and other atmospheric conditions. In the ocean, floating scientific buoys monitor atmospheric conditions near the water's surface.

Scientists also take samples of gases in the air. They

Scientists prepare to release a weather balloon.

trap air inside a container. Some containers have a pump that sucks the air through a filter. The filter contains a chemical that tests for a particular gas.

Air samples are taken at different places on the planet. One of the best places to accurately measure carbon dioxide is atop Hawaii's Mauna Loa, the world's largest volcano. The measuring station is far away from any local source of carbon dioxide pollution. Laboratory equipment analyzes the gases in the air samples.

Because of the location of Mauna Loa, it is a prime area to measure carbon dioxide.

STUDYING ANCIENT ATMOSPHERES

Like detectives looking for clues, scientists had to find clever ways of discovering what the atmosphere was like thousands of years ago. They found an answer by analyzing the air bubbles trapped in ice. Scientists use special equipment to drill ice cores from deep inside glaciers and ice sheets. The deepest ice, which formed thousands of years ago from falling snow, holds bubbles of air, chemicals, and flecks of dust. By carefully analyzing the materials trapped in an ice core, scientists can learn about temperature, precipitation, and the kinds of gases that were in the ancient lower atmosphere.

Scientists also drill cores of sediment from the seafloor and other places. Sediment cores can tell scientists where glaciers were in the past. Glaciers pick up, carry, and drop rocks and soil as they advance and retreat. Sediment samples also contain grains of ancient pollen that tell scientists what types of plants grew in an area long ago.

Another way in which scientists learn about temperature and

The European Project for Ice Coring in Antarctica

precipitation in the past is through the study of tree rings from old trees. A tree trunk grows a new ring of tissue at its center every year. The thicker a ring, the more likely that year was warm and had plenty of precipitation.

Along with other research, these studies have shown that Earth's climate has changed in the past, sometimes very suddenly. They also show that Earth's climate is changing now. According to the Environmental Protection Agency (EPA) and other organizations, such studies have confirmed that a warming trend is now occurring in both the Northern and Southern hemispheres, over land and over the oceans.

A tree's rings give scientists evidence of past weather patterns.

Global Warming and the Rain Forest

The IPCC, a United Nations agency, reports that global warming is being caused not only by burning fossil fuels but also by cutting and burning trees, especially in the tropical rain forests. Burning the trees releases more carbon dioxide into the atmosphere, and cutting down trees means there are fewer trees to remove carbon dioxide from the atmosphere.

An IPCC report in 2001 warned that if people keep adding greenhouse gases at the present rate, carbon dioxide levels could rise to between 75 percent and 350 percent above what they were at the start of the Industrial Revolution. This increase could cause the average global temperature to rise by 2.5 to 10.4 degrees (1.4 to 5.8 C) by 2100.

The world's rain forests are vital for changing carbon dioxide into oxygen.

CHAPTER SIX

Effects of Global Warming ⊕

VAST SHEETS OF ice cover Antarctica, a frozen continent at the southern end of Earth. Thick ice forms over the Arctic Ocean around the North Pole every winter. The sheets of ice around the North and South poles are called the polar ice caps. What would happen if these huge ice caps melted?

Global warming could affect the habitat of penguins in Antarctica.

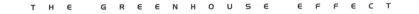

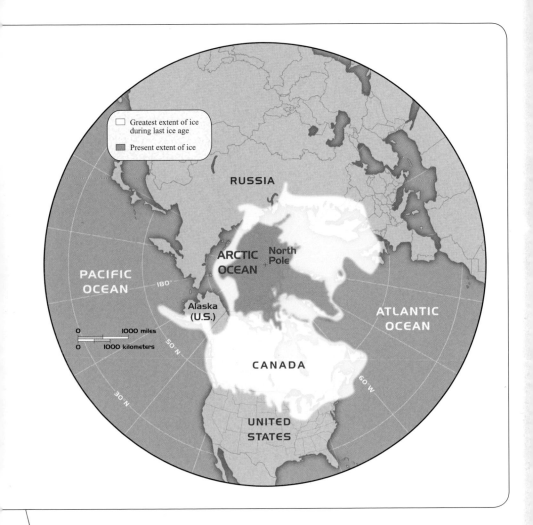

Greatest extent of ice
during last ice age

Present extent of ice

RUSSIA

ARCTIC
OCEAN

North
Pole

PACIFIC
OCEAN

180°

Alaska
(U.S.)

0   1000 miles

0   1000 kilometers

50 N

ATLANTIC
OCEAN

CANADA

60 W

30 N

UNITED
STATES

In the Arctic, satellite pictures show that the ice covering
the Arctic Ocean is melting rapidly. The loss of ice is affecting
the animals and the people living there. For example, scien-

The amount of ice on Earth between ice ages varies greatly.

tists in 2006 found walrus pups stranded in ocean water. The pups usually live on sea ice close to shore. The melting ice could make the global warming problem worse because the darker ocean waters absorb more heat.

It is difficult for scientists to predict the effects of global warming, but one effect they fear is a rise in sea levels brought about by the melting Antarctic ice cap, which covers the Antarctic continent. Measurements show that sea levels around the world have risen between 4 and 8 inches (10 and 20 cm) since the early 1900s. Rain and snowfall on land has also increased.

WATCHING FOR MELTING ICE CAPS

Scientists attribute the measurable decrease of ice in the Arctic Circle to the increased greenhouse effect. They also track icebergs that break off from Antarctica, trying to determine whether more ice is breaking away because of an increased greenhouse effect.

One of the biggest bergs was a block of ice the size of Connecticut that broke off of Antarctica in 2000. Scientists named the giant iceberg B15 and placed instruments on it to monitor where it goes and how it melts. Soon after the iceberg formed, it broke into many smaller icebergs. Rather than melting slowly, one of these icebergs suddenly shattered into pieces.

Scientists think that water on its surface seeped into cracks in the ice and broke the berg apart. They want to know whether this is a normal occurrence. They also want to know whether such a sudden disappearance of large amounts of ice could cause a sudden rise in the level of seas all over the world.

Melting icebergs have been cause for concern for many environmental scientists.

MANY UNKNOWNS

Scientists create computer models that try to predict how adding greenhouse gases may change the climate. Many factors, such as clouds and heat-reflecting aerosols, make their job more complex. In addition, global warming is likely to affect different regions in unknown ways.

How much heat and carbon dioxide can the oceans absorb? Could melting ice and an increase in water lead to increased snowfall in cold climates? Could such an increase in snowfall lead to the formation of new glaciers and bring on a new ice age instead of a warmer planet? How would global warming affect public health? Would changes in regional climates lead to more or different diseases?

Scientists also debate the effects of water vapor. Some scientists think water vapor is a more important greenhouse gas than carbon dioxide. Other scientists point out that amounts of water vapor vary from place to place and from time to time. They say water vapor is important to local weather but is not a major factor in global warming.

CONTROVERSY AND UNCERTAINTY

Some groups do not believe there is enough evidence to support the idea of global warming. They believe the increase in global temperature is part of a normal cycle and will not cause any future problems. These groups oppose taking any measures to reduce carbon dioxide output. They say that reducing emissions would be costly and harm the economy. While some scientists say the benefits of our industrialized society are far greater than the uncertain risks of global warming, others say the risk of not controlling greenhouse gas emissions is too great to wait until all the questions are answered.

A river was created from melting ice at the base of Briksdal Glacier in Briksdalen, Norway.

Is Global Warming All Bad?

Some people believe global warming is not all bad, and others believe it is actually good. A group in Russia called the Subtropical Russia Movement, for example, believes that global warming is a good thing. Members of this movement believe that global warming will bring "eternal summer" to the cold and snowy parts of their land. In fact, they want more done to bring about global warming quickly.

The Greening Earth Society, a U.S. group, argues that increased carbon dioxide is good for plants. Because plants use carbon dioxide in photosynthesis for producing their own food, the society believes that more CO_2 will lead to faster-growing, better plants. They do not believe that carbon dioxide should even be classified as a pollutant.

The rise in carbon dioxide may be beneficial for plants.

The EPA, the IPCC, and other scientific organizations agree that Earth's global climate is growing warmer because of human activities. They want governments to set up more research projects. They believe more must be learned about the enhanced greenhouse effect and its role in global climate change in order to predict what the effects will be.

Scientists study an iceberg in Antarctica.

aerosols—particles of dust or other pollutants in the atmosphere

atmosphere—the blanket of gases that surrounds a planet

climate—conditions in the atmosphere in a particular place over long periods of time

continental drift—the movement of continents from one place to another by the motion of gigantic plates that make up Earth's crust

fossil fuels—fuels, including coal, oil, and natural gas, made from the remains of ancient organisms

glaciers—large masses of slowly moving ice

global warming—rise in the average worldwide temperature of the troposphere

greenhouse gases—gases in a planet's atmosphere that trap heat energy from the sun

ice age—a period of time when Earth was covered in ice; the last ice age ended about 11,500 years ago

icebergs—floating blocks of ice that broke off from an ice sheet or glacier at the edge of the ocean

ice caps—covering of ice at the North and South poles

Industrial Revolution—a period from the middle 1700s to the 1800s of social and economic changes that took place during a transition from an agricultural and commercial society to an industrial society

infrared rays—heat rays; a form of radiation similar to visible light that is given off by all warm objects

interglacial period—warm times between ice ages

meteorologists—scientists who study weather

molecules—small bits of matter made of two or more atoms bonded together

stratosphere—layer of the atmosphere above the troposphere, rising about 31 miles (50 km)

troposphere—layer of the atmosphere closest to Earth, extending 5 to 9 miles (8 to 14.5 km) above the surface

weather—conditions in the atmosphere at a particular place and time

▸ The 1883 eruption of Krakatoa, a volcano in Indonesia, sent so much dust into the atmosphere that it may have been the cause of lower temperatures around the world for about five years.

▸ Albedo is the percentage of light reflected from a surface. Albedo is important in the study of global warming, because scientists need to know how much solar energy is absorbed by Earth's surface and how much is reflected. Light surfaces, such as ice sheets and cloud tops, have a higher percentage of albedo than dark surfaces, such as bare ground.

▸ *Voyager 1* and *Voyager 2* are the names of two space probes that visited Jupiter, Saturn, Uranus, and Neptune. The pictures and measurements the two spacecraft radioed back to Earth told astronomers much about the gases in the atmospheres of these planets.

▸ Methane, a greenhouse gas in the atmosphere, comes from natural sources as well as human activities. For example, scientists estimate that the digestive processes of termites produce about 11 percent of the natural methane sent into the atmosphere each year.

▸ Scientists have not found life on any other planet in our solar system, but they have found signs of weather. With the exceptions of Mercury and Pluto, all planets have enough gases in their atmosphere to have storms. Fierce winds on Mars, for example, create enormous dust storms.

▸ You don't have to travel north or south to experience climate changes if you live near a mountain. The higher you climb up a mountainside, the colder the climate becomes. For example, in Palm Springs, California, visitors experience a dramatic temperature change as an aerial tram takes them up a hill more than 8,500 feet (2,580 m) above the Palm Springs valley floor. In winter, the valley is warm enough for golf and hiking. At the top of the tram, however, visitors can ski and go snowshoeing.

Krakatoa erupted a cloud of dust and ash that covered the sky.

At the Library

Bradley, Susanne. *Global Warming.* North Mankato, Minn.: Stargazer Books, 2006.

Edmonds, Alex. *The Greenhouse Effect.* Brookfield, Conn.: Copper Beech Books, 1997.

Parks, Peggy J. *Global Warming.* San Diego: KidHaven Press, 2004.

Stein, R. Conrad. *The Industrial Revolution: Manufacturing a Better America.* Berkeley Heights, N.J.: Enslow Publishers, Inc., 2006.

On the Web

For more information on The Greenhouse Effect, use FactHound to track down Web sites related to this book.
1. Go to *www.facthound.com*
2. Type in this book ID: 075651956X
3. Click on the *Fetch It* button.
FactHound will find the best Web sites for you.

On the Road

National Ice Core Laboratory
    Building 810
    Denver Federal Center
    Lakewood, CO 80215
    303/202-4830

Expedition Earth
    Rochester Museum &
    Science Center
    657 East Ave.
    Rochester, NY 14607
    585/271-1880

Explore all the Earth Science books

Erosion: How Land Forms, How It Changes
    ISBN: 0-7565-0854-1

The Greenhouse Effect: Warming the Planet
    ISBN: 0-7565-1956-X

Minerals: From Apatite to Zinc
    ISBN: 0-7565-0855-X

Natural Resources: Using and Protecting Earth's Supplies
    ISBN: 0-7565-0856-8

Plate Tectonics: Earth's Moving Crust
    ISBN: 0-7565-1957-8

Soil: Digging Into Earth's Vital Resource
    ISBN: 0-7565-0857-6

A complete list of Exploring Science titles is available on our Web site: *www.compasspointbooks.com*

2/13 ⑧